History

This book is about the myths of peoples in the American Southwest who came to be called Indians. Among them were many great artists and artisans, wise observers and deep thinkers, song makers and story tellers, workers of the soil, and fine builders.

Let us try to discover how their myths arose.

Perhaps as much as 50,000 years ago, many peoples from Asia migrated across the Bering Strait and occupied the Americas. For aeons a land bridge existed where now water separates the two continents.

No one knows how long the early immigrants remained in the north, but some of them, working southward, passed through or remained in what is known as the American Southwest. Archaeologists call them Paleo-Indians, the "Ancient Indians" who used stone tools.

Slowly, environmental changes occurred. Extended drought caused large game animals to disappear. The Indians began to hunt small game, to trap, and to collect more wild plant foods. They banded together in large family groups, traveling under the guidance of a respected leader, a headman.

The Indians peopling the Americas had no means of writing as we do, so they had to observe happenings and remember them. Signs and symbols were engraved, pecked, or painted on cliff faces or cave walls. But story telling was the major way of transmitting culture history and practices from one generation to those following.

Caribou

Wild Corn (actual size) from Tehuacan Valley, Mexico
After Mangelsdorf, MacNeish, and Galinat, 1967 : 200

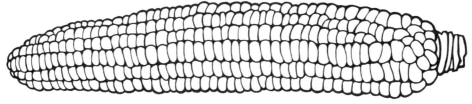

Modern Indian Corn

Nomadic life was slowly replaced by seasonal settlement and the beginnings of agriculture. Raising corn created the need for living in a fixed location, for becoming sedentary. This cultivation of corn, or *maize*, started some 5,000 years ago.

Weather became of increasing importance. With mounting respect for the sun, the headmen more than ever became sun-watchers, and they assumed growing roles in directing daily activities which centered around the wondrous plant, corn.

The growth and development of corn, tended for millennia by hand and digging stick, gave the emerging farmers new concepts. Corn and the earth itself became sacred. Anchored by corn, homes became permanent. Camps grew into settlements, and the beginning of villages was under way.

A dream of corn
After C.C. Di Peso, 1956 : 435

Myths & Legends of the

Indians
of the
Southwest

By Bertha Dutton & Caroline Olin

Book I

Navajo, Pima, Apache

(Book II, Myths & Legends of the Hopi, Acoma, Tewa, Zuñi, is also available.)

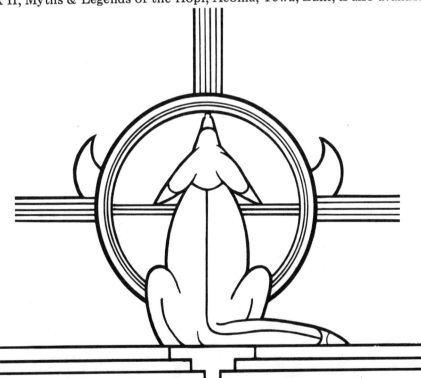

Bellerophon Books, 36 Anacapa Street, Santa Barbara, Ca 93101

Hunters following large game animals, perhaps unknowingly,
migrated from Asia across the Bering Strait to the Americas

Adapted from C. Ogburn, Jr. 1970 : 92

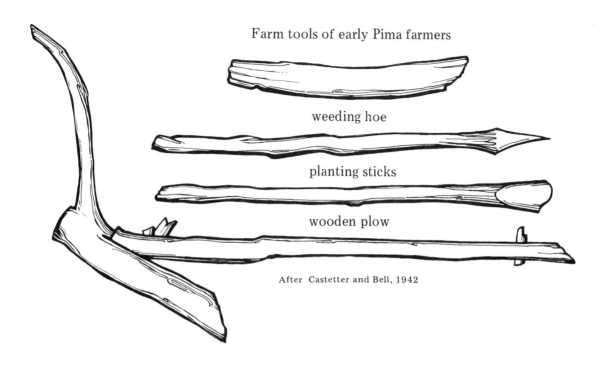

Farm tools of early Pima farmers

weeding hoe

planting sticks

wooden plow

After Castetter and Bell, 1942

The continuous attention to corn gave rise to ceremonial rites. The sun-watcher, vested with powers above those of ordinary people, became the spiritual leader of emerging religious ideas. He portrayed the sun as supreme father of mankind and all lesser forms of life, and the earth as mother. The people became familiar with deities in visible form, Sun Father and Earth Mother. Rays of the sun impregnated the earth, and from such a miraculous union, celestial offspring were born—usually twins, twin boys.

A Pima farmer using a wooden hoe

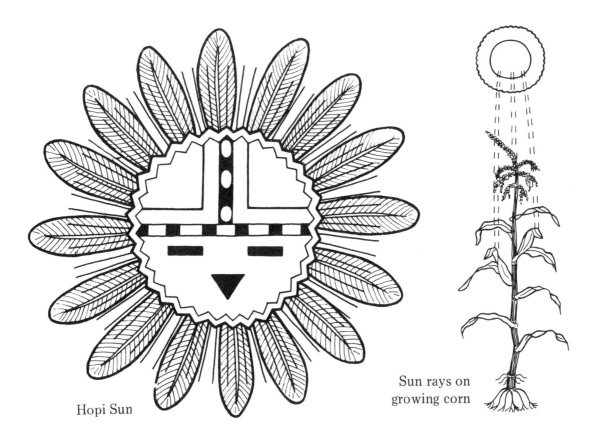

Hopi Sun

Sun rays on
growing corn

The sun-watcher chose assistants to help him. Each assistant was given specific duties and obligations. From such simple origin, priesthoods and ceremonialism came into the Indian culture.

As Indians depicted manifestations of supernatural personages, elders began to tell their children how all things came to be. Telling took place during ceremonial observances, or when families gathered around flickering fires on chilly nights following the harvest season. As the stories passed from generation to generation, folk history was made. Myths and legends, like parables in the Holy Bible and other sacred books, enabled priests and their officials to bring knowledge and understanding, law and order, into the life of the people.

Mother Earth symbol

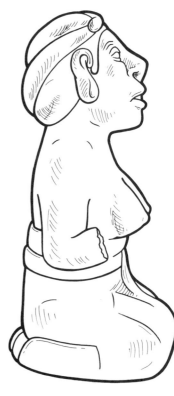

Aztec Corn Goddess

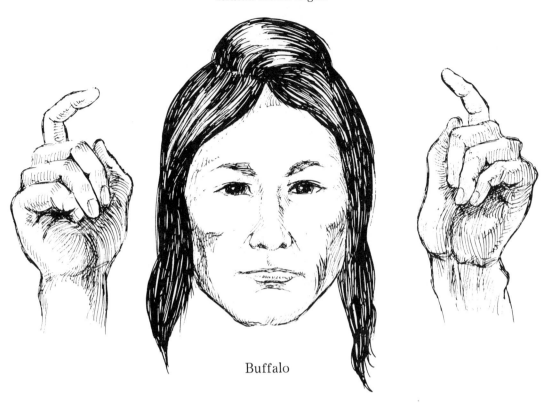

Buffalo

Aside from reading Indian stories and myths for pleasure, we can use such sources as tools for learning bits of unrecorded history and for providing understanding of the Indian way of thinking or doing daily tasks. Personages who represent celestial bodies or supernatural beings, places mentioned in the wanderings, the wild life (plants, animals, insects, birds) with which early Indians were familiar, and color symbols may make it possible to identify locations and periods in which myths were set. Implements used in the stories help tell whether the Indians were hunters and gatherers or farmers, whether the level of culture was high or low, whether government was simple or complex, whether religious concepts were rudimentary or advanced.

The tales and myths recited—if they are heard first-hand or obtained from reliable informants—can be counted upon as being true for some distance back in time. Then comes a point when tales "the old ones" told are repeated more or less faithfully. Farther back, the stories become increasingly mythical. They become dimmer and less complete.

Bear

Antelope

The Piman-Speaking Indians—Background

Indians differ as much as does a Spaniard from a German, or an Englishman from an Arab: alike to a great extent, yet dissimilar in some ways. Archeologists recognize the American Southwest—southern California, Arizona, New Mexico, southwestern Colorado, parts of Utah, southern Nevada, and northernmost Mexico —as a distinct area, wherein Indians speaking different languages attained many cultural similarities. The area where the states of Utah, New Mexico, Arizona and Colorado share a common boundary point—the only place in the U.S.A. where four corners touch—is called the Four Corners Region.

In the semi-arid desert lands of southern Arizona, a sub-area called the Hohokam has been distinguished. The most revealing excavations of Hohokam culture have been made at a site near Phoenix, Arizona, called Snaketown, or "the place of snakes." From evidence found, it is believed that people in significant numbers came from Mexico and settled there some 2,200 years ago.

Many of the workers who assisted with the Snaketown excavations were Piman Indians—Pima (river people) and Papago (of the desert south of the Pima). Both scientists and the Indians believe that the Pimans may be descendants of the Hohokam peoples. The name Hohokam is Piman, meaning "Things all used up," or "Those who have gone."

Since the Pimans may have as long a history as any of the known peoples in the area, we turn to their myths and stories first. These Indians lived, not in communal pueblos, but on small ranches *(rancherias)* in separate family dwellings. Several such ranch settlements are considered a village.

Papago territory once stretched from the mountains of Mexico into the Arizona desert. In that location the Papago were the northernmost of all Indians known to have spoken a language related to that of the Aztecs of Mexico,who were conquered by the Spaniards. This language, which was spoken over a wide area, is called Uto-Aztecan. It is not surprising that the Papago used words of old Aztec prayers. They also had folk tales, games, and ceremonies which echoed those of the extinct Aztec Indians.

Contemporary Papago basketry bowls

In the past, each Papago village had an elderly officer who—under various names—was considered the earthly representative of deity. His hereditary function was to look after his people and to teach them the Papago way. A common means of doing this was to recite their cultural history, which was preserved in songs and memorized stories. Through generation after generation, before a man child was born, "a body of magic by which the ancestors ruled their world" had been accumulated. A man dreamed his songs and passed them on to his son.

The time for recitation was the four nights in winter when the Papago considered that the sun stood still—that time before the sun turned back from its southern journey (winter solstice).

Everything holy was noted in fours. On those four nights Papago men gathered in their round ceremonial house—"their holy place"—and listened to the storyteller. Their heads were bowed, their arms folded, and they sat cross-legged. This was the required position. Starting with the creation of the world, the old man talked, recited poems, and sang his songs. No one could interrupt. No one could sleep.

An omnipotent one, called Earthmaker or Earthdoctor, so the Papago storyteller recited, created the world from sweat and greasy dirt that he rubbed from his own skin. "The flat earth met the sky with a crash like that of falling rocks, and from the two was born Iitoi *(EE-ee-toy)*, the protector of the Papago." Earthmaker and Iitoi shaped and peopled the world. Coyote, "who came to life uncreated," followed them everywhere. Iitoi became the hero of Papago myths. "He was the vessel through which power passed." This power was impersonal, "a great unknown force pervading the earth."

The Papagos' kinsmen, the river-dwelling Pima, were sustained by agriculture. As told in the following stories, corn was a prized addition to their natural foods. Canals built by the ancient Hohokam Indians for irrigating their fields were being used by the Pima when first reported by white men. Some of those canals still are being used.

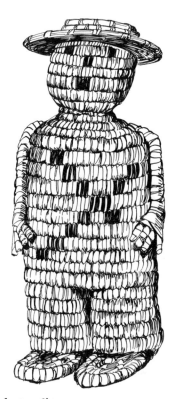

Contemporary Papago basketry figures

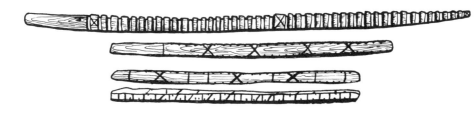

Papago Calendar Stick and other Notched Sticks

The Franciscan missionary, Marcos de Niza, came among the Pima in 1539 and introduced Christianity. Father Eusebio Francisco Kino, an energetic Italian missionary-explorer, arrived in 1687. He found the Pima to be friendly, industrious, and peaceful people who allied themselves with the Spaniards. They were receptive to Christianity and came to live under the missionary system.

But strong non-Indian influence greatly affected their culture. By the beginning of the 20th century, the Pima had ceased to grow cotton, which formerly they had dyed and woven. All trace of their aboriginal dress had vanished; little evidence of old customs remained. Ceremonies and dances were no longer held.

Papago Skipping Dance

The Pima youth had little knowledge of their own songs. It had been the custom to name the dance songs after birds. An early recorder of Pima music found an old Holy Man *(cacique—cah-SEE-kay)* who still remembered the songs of his people. Although the cacique told the recorder that no man on their reservation dared to sing in that day, he allowed the creation myth and its songs to be recorded. The old man was encouraged to sing, and was told that "when a man sings we know his heart is happy."

Recently, with pride in being an Indian awakening again, the Pima—and the Papago also—have revived interest in their attire of the past and in their dances. As a result, they present some colorfully costumed dances, such as a basket dance, a stick dance, bird dances, and others. Conditions similar to this are found with most of the Indian peoples of the Southwest.

It is said that in olden times the Pima and the Papago had the same religion and the same ceremonies. Like the Papago, the river-dwelling Pima do not relate myths during the summertime. If they did, they might be bitten by rattlesnakes (which hibernate during the winter). Certain traditional features of the myths are given with great exactness. When recited under ceremonial situations, the myths go on—or used to—night after night.

In the Pima tellings that follow, only brief excerpts can be given. As in the folk history of any Indian people, myths and tales relate to every event that took place in Piman life.

Pima basketry design

After A. E. Robinson, 1954 : 22

Creation Story

In a Pima version of the creation myth recited at the very beginning of the 20th century, Earthmaker, wandering around in nowhere, rubbed the sweat and dirt from his breast. He made a tiny ball which he held out on the palm of his hand. The ball tipped over three times. The fourth time it stayed straight "in the middle of the air and there it remains now as the world."

Earthmaker then created the first bush; it was greasewood, or creosotebush. He made tiny red ants to live on the bush, to live on the gum that comes from its stem. The tiny red ants did no good, so white ants were created. They worked and enlarged the earth. They kept making the earth larger and larger. At last it was big enough to make a resting place for Earthmaker.

Pima Basket Dance

Buzzard

Next, it is said, a Person was created. Earthmaker made him out of his eye, "out of the shadow of his eyes, to assist him, to be like him, and to help him in creating trees and human beings and everything that was to be on the earth." This person was named Buzzard. He was given all power, but he did not do the work for which he was created. So Earthmaker himself created the mountains and everything that has seed and is good to eat. For if he had created human beings first they would have had nothing to live on.

But, after making Buzzard and before he made the mountains and seed, Earthmaker made the sun. In order to do this he first made water, which he placed in a hollow earthen vessel to harden—to become ice. He placed the hardened ball in the sky. "First he placed it in the North, but it did not work; then he placed it in the West, but it did not work; then he placed it in the South, but it did not work; then he placed it in the East and there it worked as he wanted it to."

He made the moon in the same way and tried it in the same places, with the same results. When he made the stars, "he took the water in his mouth and spurted it up into the sky. But the first night his stars did not give light enough. So he took the doctor-stone (a crystal or quartz pebble) and smashed it up, and took the pieces and threw them into the sky to mix with the water in the stars, and then there was enough light."

Man and Woman Story

Earthmaker again rubbed his breast and from the rubbings he made two little dolls. He laid them on the earth. And they were human beings, man and woman. The people increased until they filled the earth. The first parents were perfect, and there was no sickness and no death. But when the earth was full, "there was nothing to eat, so they killed and ate each other."

An Indian cradle is
usually made with a
board or other firm
material at the back.
It is a sacred thing.
Baby after baby
has found secure
comfort in its cra-
dle, or cradleboard.
At the same time,
a baby could be
with the family to
observe and learn
daily activities
—while growing
with a straight back.

Figures in human
form were made by
Indians who long
ago lived at a place
now known as Snake-
town, in Arizona.
Perhaps some of the
"dolls" of the mythi-
cal beings made by
Earthmaker, Coyote,
and Iitoi looked like
these. These were
first two rods of clay,
then partly joined to-
gether, and lastly a
rude figure.

After E. Haury, 1976 : 256

Not liking the way his people acted, Earthmaker"let the sky fall to kill them.
But when the sky dropped he, himself, took a staff and broke a hole through,
through which he and Buzzard emerged and escaped, leaving behind them all the
people dead."

Now being on top of this fallen sky, Earthmaker again made a man and a
woman in the same way as before."But this man and woman became grey when old,
and their children became grey younger still, and so on till the babies were grey in
their cradles."And Earthmaker,"who had made a new earth and sky, just as there had
been before, did not like his people becoming grey in their cradles, so he let the sky
fall on them again, and again made a hole and escaped,"with Buzzard as before.

On top of this second sky, again he made a new sky and a new earth, and new
people, just as he had before. But these new people made a vice of smoking."Before
human beings had never smoked till they were old, but now they smoked younger,
and each generation still younger, till the infants wanted to smoke in their cradles."
Earthmaker did not like this either, and so he let the sky fall again; then he created
everything anew in the same way, "and this time he created the earth as it is now."

Moon

Sun

Milky Way

Morning Star

Celestial bodies that were personified

After E. C. Parsons, 1925 : Plates 3 and 4; and A. M. Stephen, 1969 : Plate XIV

At first, "the whole slope of the world was westward, and though there were peaks rising from this slope there were no true valleys, and all the water that fell ran away and there was no water for the people to drink." Buzzard was sent to fly around among the mountains and over the earth, "to cut valleys with his wings, so that the water could be caught and distributed and there might be enough for the people to drink."

Coyote and Iitoi — the Flood

The sun was male and the moon was female. They met once a month."And the moon became a mother and went to a mountain called Sun Striking Mountain." There her baby was born. Mother Moon had her duties to perform. She had "to turn around and give light, so she made a place for the child by tramping down the weedy bushes and there left it. And the child, having no milk, was nourished on the earth." This child was Coyote—thus the night-prowling beast was mothered by the moon. As he grew, he went for a walk and came to the house of Earthmaker and Buzzard. Earthmaker recognized him and called him by name, Coyote.

Coyote

Then out of the north came a powerful personage, a great unknown force pervading the earth, recognizable as Iitoi (EE-ee-toy). Buzzard and Coyote he addressed, each, as his younger brother. The two disputed this; they claimed to have been here first, and to be older than he. Iitoi was so powerful that even Earthmaker trembled before him. Finally, because he insisted so strongly, he was allowed to be called Elder Brother. He then made his home with Earthmaker, Buzzard, and Coyote, and did many wonderful things. Because of his ambition to do great deeds and get more fame, Iitoi was always trying to outdo Earthmaker, who was kind and generous, and really the strongest.

Some of the undertakings of Iitoi caused a great flood to cover the land. Forewarned, each of these four original ones planned means by which they could escape. When the floods came, the people fled to the mountains. They had to move higher and higher as the water rose. This happened four times. Then Earthmaker used power to help his people; he raised the mountains."But at last he saw all was to be a failure. And he called the people and asked them all to come "close together, and he took his doctor-stone or stone of light, and held it in the palm of his hand and struck it hard with his other hand, and it thundered so loud that all the people were frightened and they all turned into stone."

Little birds flew up to the sky and hung on by their bills. "The flood rose higher until it reached the woodpecker's tail, and you can see the marks on it to this day."One little bird was cold and cried so loud that the other birds pulled off their feathers and built him a nest so that he could keep warm. When he was warm he quit crying."And then the little birds sang, for they had power to make the water go down by singing, and as they sang the waters gradually receded.

When the land began to appear, Earthmaker and Coyote got out of the water. Buzzard was flying high in the sky. Iitoi was the last to get out on dry land. Even so, he argued again that he was the first, and greeted Earthmaker as 'my younger brother.' Just to please him, Earthmaker gave him his way and let him be considered the elder."All of them, even the little birds, though they knew better, admitted that Iitoi was the Elder Brother.

Note: These tales are adapted from Lloyd, J. W., 1911.)

Woodpecker

How Sickness Came

While the earth was still damp, Iitoi, Earthmaker, and Coyote took clay and began to make dolls. They did not let each other see what they were making. Earthmaker did not make good ones"because he remembered some of his people had escaped the flood through a hole in the earth, and he intended to visit them and he did not want to make anything better than they were to take the place of them."

Coyote made the poorest of all. Iitoi asked if they were ready. They said,"Yes." and all turned and showed what they had made. Iitoi asked Earthmaker why he made such queer dolls. He found fault with all of them. That made Earthmaker angry, and he began to sink into the ground. He took his greasewood stick and hooked it into the sky and pulled the sky down while he was sinking."But Iitoi spread his hand over his dolls, and held up the sky, and seeing that Earthmaker was sinking into the earth he sprang and tried to hold him and cried, 'Man, what are you doing! Are you going to leave me and my people here alone?' "

But Earthmaker slipped through his hands,"leaving in them only the waste and excretion of his skin. And that is how there is sickness and death among us." Swinging his hands, Iitoi scattered disease over all the earth. He washed his hands in a pool and the impurities remaining in the water are the source of the malarias and all the diseases of dampness.

Praying for Rain—Beginning of Rain Dance

According to old Pima custom when rain was desired, one of the leading men who knew the rain ceremony well, notified the medicine men, the reciter, and the singers. These agreed to begin the ceremony at the end of four days. On the third day one or more criers were sent to the adjoining villages to announce that on the morrow the ceremony would be held.

At eventide the leader called the names of the medicine men, and each took his position behind the lighted fire, facing toward the east. Then names of the singers were called. The leading singer sat behind the medicine men. His assistants took places on either side of him and around the fire. Finally the reciter was named, and he took his place with the medicine men. Upon the leader's announcing that it was time for the ceremony to commence, the reciter started his oration.

With traditional statements he began: "When the earth was new it was shaking and rough." In a thoughtful manner he entreated Black Mocking Bird who lives in the west, and sought his aid in controlling the earth. He said, "If your plans for controlling the earth have failed, go far hence and leave the black wind and the black clouds behind you. Your people will henceforth entreat your assistance from a distance."

He then called upon Blue Mocking Bird in the south for help. He came, and gave commands to control the hills, mountains, trees, everything. But still the earth continued shaking. So the orator said, "Yes, Blue Mocking Bird, if your plans have failed, go hence and leave the blue wind and blue clouds behind you. Your people will henceforth entreat your assistance from a distance."

Then, knowing White Mocking Bird of the east, the orator sought his assistance. White Mocking Bird also came, bringing commands for controlling the hills, mountains, trees, everything. But the earth continued shaking. The orator said, "Yes, White Mocking Bird, if your plans for controlling the earth have failed, go hence and leave the white winds and the white clouds behind you. Your people will henceforth entreat your assistance from a distance."

Rain Dancers

After R. Underhill, 1940

Building the Ceremonial House—End of the Rain Dance

After entreating the birds, the reciter said, "Above me enveloped in darkness lived the magician *Kuvik*, on whom I called for help. He came in a friendly spirit, with commands that would control the hills, mountains, trees, everything. The earth became much quieter, but still moved somewhat."

Then aid was sought from Grey Spider in the west. He came and being friendly,"took bundles of sticks, which he placed in the edges of the land and sewed them firmly together. He pulled the black corner at the west, where stands the house of the Rain god of the west. He firmly enveloped the earth with his black power. He pulled the blue corner at the south, where stands the house of the Rain god of the south. He firmly enveloped the earth with his blue power. He pulled the white corner at the east, where stands the house of the Rain god of the east. He firmly enveloped the earth with his white power, and with that the earth became quieter.

"Then in the west there was a Black Measuring Worm that was friendly to me and came in answer to my entreaty. He came in four strides and in short broken lengths stood up as crotched posts. In the south there was a Blue Measuring Worm that was friendly to me and came in answer to my entreaty. He came in four strides and in short broken lengths formed the joists to lie upon the posts. In the east there was a White Measuring Worm that was friendly to me and he came in four strides in answer to my entreaty. In short broken lengths he covered the joists with a layer of small poles. In the north there was a Reddish Measuring Worm that was friendly to me and came in four strides in answer to my entreaty. He in short broken lengths covered the other parts in a curved outer layer, thus finishing the framework.

"Then, in the west there was a Blue Gopher who came with plenty of brush which he placed layer above layer around the house, covering it as with thin clouds. Around the house were four gopher hills from which he covered it with earth in a thin, even layer, as snow covers the ground.

"Looking around the earth I selected a gopher to take me up like a little boy and place me in the house. He placed a brand of fire down before me and a [ceremonial] cigarette also. Lighting the cigarette he puffed smoke toward the east in a great white arch. The shadow of the arch crept across the earth beneath. A grassy carpet covered the earth. Scattering seed, he caused the corn with the large stalk, large leaf, full tassel, good ears to grow and ripen. Then he took it and stored it away.

"As the sun's rays extended to the plants, so our thoughts reached out to the time when we would enjoy the life-giving corn. With gladness we cooked and ate the corn and, free from hunger and want, were happy. Your worthy sons and daughters, knowing nothing of the starvation periods, have been happy. The old men and the old women will have their lives prolonged yet day after day by the possession of corn.

"People must unite in desiring rain. If it rains their land shall be as a garden, and they will not be as poor as they have been."

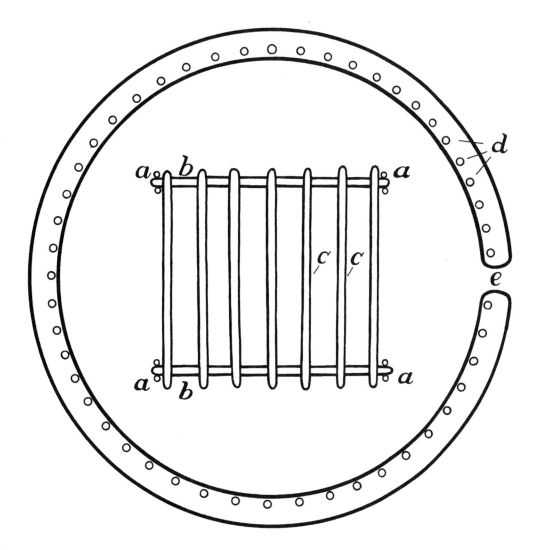

Ground plan of a Pima house

After F. Russell, 1908 : 154

Framework of an oldstyle Pima house

After F. Russell, 1908 : Pl. XXXVa

A completed Piman house
of olden day style

After F. Russell, 1908, Plate XXXV b

These illustrations show how the Measuring Worm myth served to instruct children. Hearing this tale, time and again, one would learn how to build a traditional Piman home or ceremonial structure. Each bit of material necessary for the construction is mentioned. Every step of the building is named in order and in a legendary way its significance is explained. Remembering the myth a young man would know that he should call on friends to help erect his own home. He would know the materials to assemble and the procedures to be followed.

A ceremonial meeting in
a Papago holy place

After R. Underhill, 1940 : 30

The Anasazi potters painted life forms to a limited degree, such as shown on these vessels which were excavated from ruins located in the Four Corners area. They were made in early Pueblo times, between A.D. 450 and 750.

Early Pueblo Bowls
excavated on a Navajo Reservation

After E. H. Morris.

THE NAVAJO

Although the Navajo were the last of the Indian groups to settle in the Southwest, they are increasing rapidly. Now they number more than 150,000, the largest Indian tribe in the U.S.A. They dwell on some 18,000,000 acres of reservation and leased semi-desert lands in the Four Corners Region. The Navajo speak a language called Athabascan, which is unrelated to the tongues spoken by earlier inhabitants of the Southwest.

Since they had no books, no writing, their myths and legends were carried in memory from generation to generation. Some of their knowledge was made visible by depictions pecked or painted on rocky cliff walls and through sandpaintings. Usually the tales were based on events and episodes in the lives of deities and heroes. The sacred myths also describe how ceremonial chants began and how they must be performed.

From a Navajo petroglyph panel carved on a sandstone cliff; Crow Canyon, New Mexico

A Navajo Story of Creation

According to an old Navajo medicine man called Very Tall One, in the beginning the Holy People came up from below— the underworld—to the Fourth World. All was dark in this lowest world, the night world. No light from the sun or stars existed; color took the place of light. The original spirit being was First Man and the second, First Woman.

Petroglyph showing Pueblo influence
in Blanco Canyon, Old Navajoland

Black Ant, created by First Man, was told, "You are made the first person in this black world for the purpose of bringing up by prayer other people into the brighter world." (Today ants never blink; they even sleep with their eyes open. This is because they were born in the black world and had to keep their eyes open all the time).

The first word ever spoken was when Black Ant said "Mother" to First Woman—thus, Fourth World was called One Word World. Black Ant floated upward on water that kept rising higher. He was able to dig twelve days and twelve nights until he reached the world above, the Third World.

That Third World, where earth and water existed, was dim and bluish, which represents the blue skies of today. Here Red Ant, Black Ant's younger brother, was born, but they could not understand each other since they had only one word. First

Black Ant and Red Ant dig through into the next world

Woman taught the ants to say "Father," and then the Third World was called Two Words World.

By taking turns for twelve days and nights, when the waters began to rise again, the ants dug through until they came into a dim yellowish world, which represents the yellow that comes just after sunset, the Second World. Here it was barely light, just enough to see. They were at last able to see the Holy People who had made them. They also met their ant relatives, insects which had stings, and a coyote, also made by First Beings. They were told that black is for night, the time to sleep; that they should sleep until the light comes up from the east, the white of daybreak; and that they should stay awake when they see the blue of the sky and the yellow of the sunset.

From a painting by A.V. Tsinajinnie, a Navajo artist.

The first Navajo hogan, supported by forked sticks, had five poles, one from the west, one from the south, one from the north, and two from the east at the doorway. In the first hogan at the east lived the first headman, who gave wisdom to the people. The deities, called *ye'ii* (YAY-ee-ee), taught the people to live in a peaceful way, but Wolf argued with Mountain Lion and his wife. As a consequence all the men and all the women separated for a time until they realized they could not be complete without each other.

Coyote, a mischief maker, saw Water Monster's babies, Water Boy and Water Girl, floating in a whirl of "the waters that cross" and decided to steal them. Soon a great wave topped with white foam began rising and coming toward the people. No one seemed able to stop it.

Little White Pine Squirrel grew a pine tree for the people to climb above the waters, but it did not work, so the squirrel came down. Next Black Squirrel tried to grow a spruce tree, but it only grew as high as it grows today, so he came down. Then the common squirrel tried his tree, the piñon, but that did not grow even as high as the spruce. Garter Snake tried with a little plant about a meter high called Big Seed Grass, or lamb's-quarter. Chameleon tried to grow a low plant with yellow flowers. Rock Lizard's plant was just a little thing, a salt weed with thorns. All was to no avail.

Just before darkness settled the people saw the flood come up to them. Frightened, they prayed and made offerings. The water rose almost to the sacred hogan in the east.

The first Navajo house—"hogan made of rainbows," which belonged to "Man wrapped in a Rainbow."

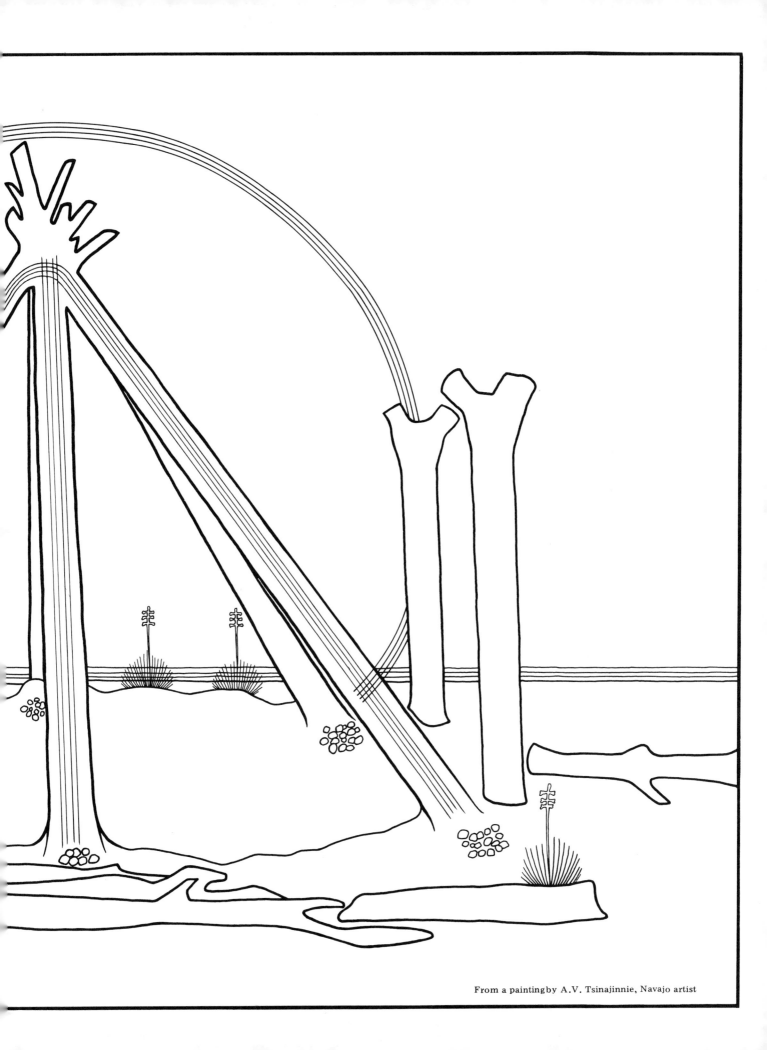

From a painting by A.V. Tsinajinnie, Navajo artist

They knew if the water covered the hogans of the Holy People it meant the end of all things. However, two beings, the black and the white flute-blowers who do not talk, motioned the people to go into the four holes on the sides of their flutes. Each flute drew in the people according to the color of their skin. As the flute-blowers blew, the flutes began to grow and grew higher until they could grow no more.

The flute-players looked out and said, "This is a dangerous place. There is nothing in this world but a monstrous Grebe who controls this water and does not let anybody live here. Can anyone talk him into letting you live here?" Said Coyote: "I'm smart enough." But the people picked Locust to go out and talk with Grebe. This monster tried to put out Locust's eyes with two arrows, but Locust did not blink.'Even today the locust does not blink, and if you try to stick anything sharp in his eye it will just go off to one side.'

Grebe said, "If you can swallow these arrows like I can, you can come up." But Locust said, "That's nothing—anybody can do that. But if you can do this, I won't come up," and he thrust both arrows through his body, taking them out at opposite ends. When Grebe, the water being, saw this he knew that Locust had more power than he, and the people gained the right to come up to the First World, our present world.

When the water reached the top of the flute, Water Monster and his wife were there, and they demanded their babies back. They were returned, and the waters subsided. The Navajo came out of the white flute and the Hopi came out of the black flute. Wind drained the water away, but the earth was still so soft

Coyote Steals Water Monster's Babies, Water Boy and Water Girl

From a painting by A.V. Tsinajinnie, a Navajo artist.

and muddy that when Badger tried to walk on it, his legs went down into the mud. (Even today badgers have this black marking.)Turkey was the last one in the flute. When he came out, he shook from under his wings all kinds of seed he had taken with him from the world below, and they were planted in this, the First World.

Black God, the Fire God, had been given control over fire. He guarded it selfishly. Four times the people begged Black God to give them fire for their hogan. While they were discussing this, Coyote stole the fire and brought it to the main hogan, and all the other people got little fires from it.

One day the wife of Mountain Lion was missing. Her tracks were found leading to the edge of a hole. Mountain Lion looked down into the hole and saw her sitting combing her hair. His shadow fell on the ground beside her and a mouse ran to the woman. This signified bad luck. The woman looked up and said, "You shall return to where I am when you die." The people realized this was death; she had died and returned to the Second World.

With dirt brought with them from below, the Holy People created the four sacred mountains. A baby girl was found wrapped in a cloud in fog on top of a mountain, now called Gobernador Knob. The baby was to become Changing Woman, the Navajo mother deity, who symbolizes rejuvenation of the earth as the seasons change. Coyote pulled out a sacred ritual "cigarette" half yellow and half white. The yellow represents summer and the white winter (snow).

The Emergence of the Navajo

The Sun and Moon were made and became deities. For each a special song was sung. Sun was made with blue shell laid upon a sacred buckskin from the skin of a deer that had never been shot. To make light First Man had two crystals. Scum from

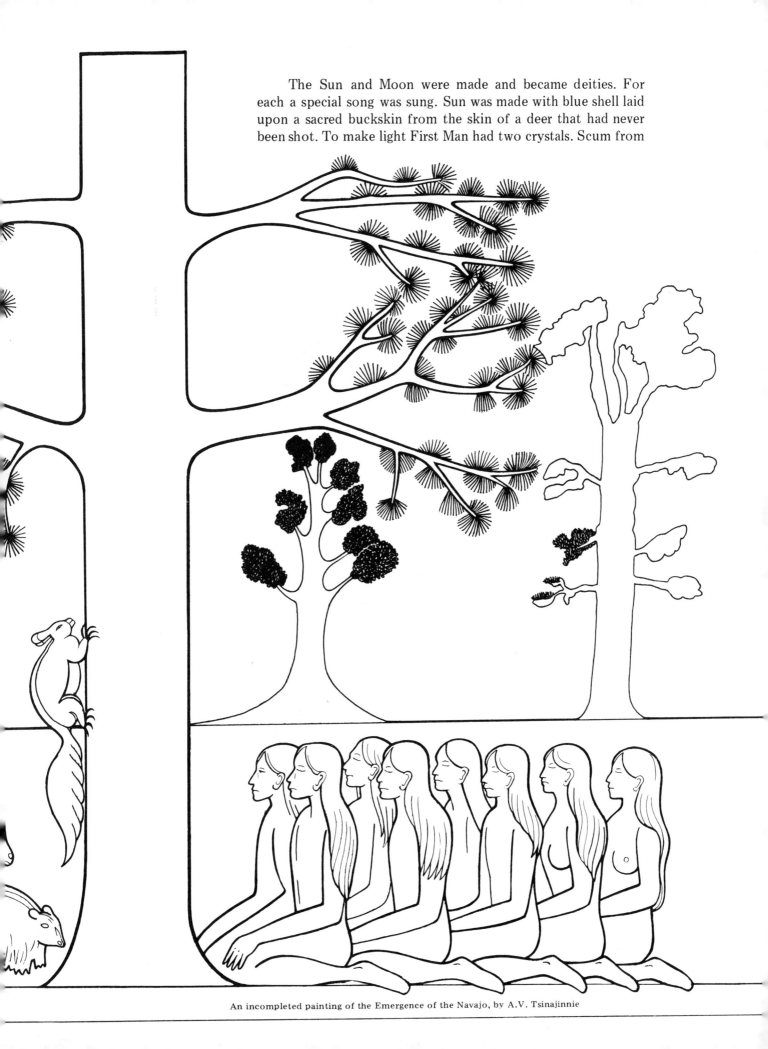

An incompleted painting of the Emergence of the Navajo, by A.V. Tsinajinnie

water was dabbed over them so the crystals might stick, and Sun was covered with the heated crystal. Red feathers were put around Sun, surrounded by a rainbow. Encircling Sun were circles of blue, then black, yellow, sparkling (pink), and lastly red. The feathers in the center were covered by these colors. The being who carried the white flute and had led the people up from beneath was asked to carry the sun, the light, each day.

Some of the crystal was left over. It was made into the dippers and stars, which Coyote hurled, scattering them up in the heavens. The rest of the leftover powder he spread between the main stars to form the Milky Way. White shell covered the face of Moon and gave it a shiny look. The decoration for Moon was the same as for Sun,

only the feathers were white, and the streaks hiding the feathers were: white first, second yellow, then black, sparkling (pink), and red last.

When all the world was complete a ritual was held. Then the *ye'ii* (all the Holy People: First Man, First Woman, Changing Woman, Sun, Moon, Talking God, Calling God, even Coyote, and many others) got upon Evening Star to depart. They told the people, "This is the last time you will see us, but we will send back the sacred birds to you." And today you see many of the sacred birds, the bluebirds, yellow birds, and others. (You will realize that the Holy People of the Navajo are comparable to the Katsinas of the Pueblo Indians*—see Volume II.)

The How and Why of Sandpaintings

It is believed that the Navajo and Apache learned from the Pueblo Indians to make sandpaintings. Some of the paintings were fitted to their own myths and to ones borrowed from the Pueblos. The Navajo did not adopt the idea of having a permanent ceremonial chamber—a kiva. Not having a room with vertical walls, they made their paintings on the flat ground. With developing myths they had opportunities to carry the sandpainting art to heights differing from the restricted practices of Pueblo ceremonialism.

When the Holy People taught Bead Boy to make sandpaintings, they strictly forbade reproduction of them in permanent form. It was insisted that when sandpaintings were made, every detail must be exactly as originally prescribed; an incorrect or imperfect painting would result in an unsuccessful cure. As a result, all knowledge of the designs is carried in memory by medicine men. Photography and sketching are forbidden. Few reproductions have been made by the Navajo, for they fear disapproval of the Holy People. Certain white people have been able to memorize sandpainting designs and have recreated them, and had them checked for correctness by friendly medicine men informants.

Sandpaintings are made for specific purposes and to enlist the aid of supernaturals, the Holy People. Functions of the paintings are to cure illnesses; to bless people, animals, events, and hogans or special structures; and to create and restore harmony between man and nature.

Sandpaintings (sometimes called drypaintings—for not all materials used are sand) are made by trickling dry pulverized pigments between thumb and forefinger. These are chiefly red, yellow, and white sands from natural sandstone, black charcoal, colored cornmeals, crushed flower petals, and plant pollens. They are placed on a smooth layer of desert sand on the earth floor of a hogan or out of doors. Sometimes buckskin or cloth is used as a background. Made by a chanter (medicine man), with a few assistants or as many as forty, a painting may be a few centimeters in size or as large as several meters across. A chanter with four to six assistants usually requires three to five hours to complete an average painting. Then, after a painting is used ceremonially, it is destroyed immediately.

In the Bead Chant myth the boy out hunting alone for food was having a hard time. After a series of misfortunes, Bead Boy gained supernatural assistance, protection, and power. He returned home bringing with him knowledge of ritualistic lore and paraphernalia which he taught to his brother for the benefit of earth people, before he departed to live with the Holy People.

Such myths are hero stories; they show the dangers of life and the means of warding off and counteracting them. They also show the way in which the hero acquires control over the forces of his environment and the process of growth from childhood to adult status: ties and separation from his family to undertake his own hunting adventure, the acceptance of discipline, participation and endurance to learn a long ritual, reconciliation with his family and his gift to them of his ritual knowledge—all steps in assuming the responsibilities of an adult role in society. Navajo art and myth embody this motivation of social values.

Bead Chant Myth

Bead Boy, or Scavenger the Beggar Boy, mythical hero of the Beadway ceremony, was taken captive by the Hopi Spider People. Despite warnings uttered by his parents not to go off into certain places alone, Bead Boy disobediently went off hunting alone for rabbits and seeds into an area along the San Juan River.

There the Pueblo Indians forced him into a basket and lowered him from the top of a high cliff into an eagles' nest on a ledge far below. They wanted eagle feathers and demanded that Bead Boy deliver two eaglets from the nest to them. They fully intended to leave Bead Boy stranded there. The Hopi Butterfly People asked him to go with them, but Big Fly, Navajo messenger, told him, "No."

Wind heard these plans and swiftly carried the message to Talking God and Calling God, Navajo deities who warned the boy not to steal the eaglets. When the parent eagles came back to their nest and discovered what was happening, they fed Bead Boy and gave him drink, in gratitude for his not taking the eaglets. For four days they brought him cooked corn in packets attached to their breasts and water in hollow reeds fastened to their tails.

By lifting Bead Boy up to their home in the sky, they saved him from the hostile Pueblo people who were attacking the nest from above. His face was painted with white clay and he was wrapped in a dark cloud tied by lightnings and lifted with raincords. Inside the cloud a rock crystal gave him light. He was able to breathe through a yellow reed that whistled every time he took a breath. The birds, hawks and eagles, all joined together to lift Bead Boy to the sky. On the way, moisture from the cloud dampened their wings and caused them to tire. They begged aid from the feathered arrowsnakes who then assisted them through the skyhole. (The Navajo believe that arrowsnakes, "racers," can soar.)

Bead Boy lived with the eagles for some time and experienced many adventures and dilemmas. By disobeying the eagles' instructions he was shot at by frogs and bad eagles, and captured by Spider. Once he was trapped by rocks but the hunting animals, White Wolf, Black Spotted Lion, Yellow Mountain Lion, Blue Lynx, and Variegated Badger dug him out. In return he was able to help his protectors by saving the eagles in fights with enemy bees, tumble weeds, rocks, and grass.

As a result the eagles offered him a marriage, taught him their paintings, songs, prayers, and other ceremonial knowledge required for the Beadway ceremony. In order to travel back to earth he was fitted with a feather cloak and wings, which gave him the power of sky-flying creatures.

On earth Bead Boy saw that the Spider People who had forced him into the eagles' nest were suffering from sores caused by the eaglets' feathers shaken down upon the Pueblo people when they stormed the nest with flaming arrows. (Beadway is sung mainly to cure skin irritations and head afflictions, and is associated with lameness.) After he taught his brother to be a medicine man of the Beadway ceremony and how to cure the Pueblo people, Bead Boy ascended to the sky in his bird garments. The desperate Spider People promised to pay his brother some wonderful dancing beads if he would cure them in a ceremony.

Sandpainting from the Bead Chant: Bead Boy in Eagle's Nest   After G. Reichard, 1939

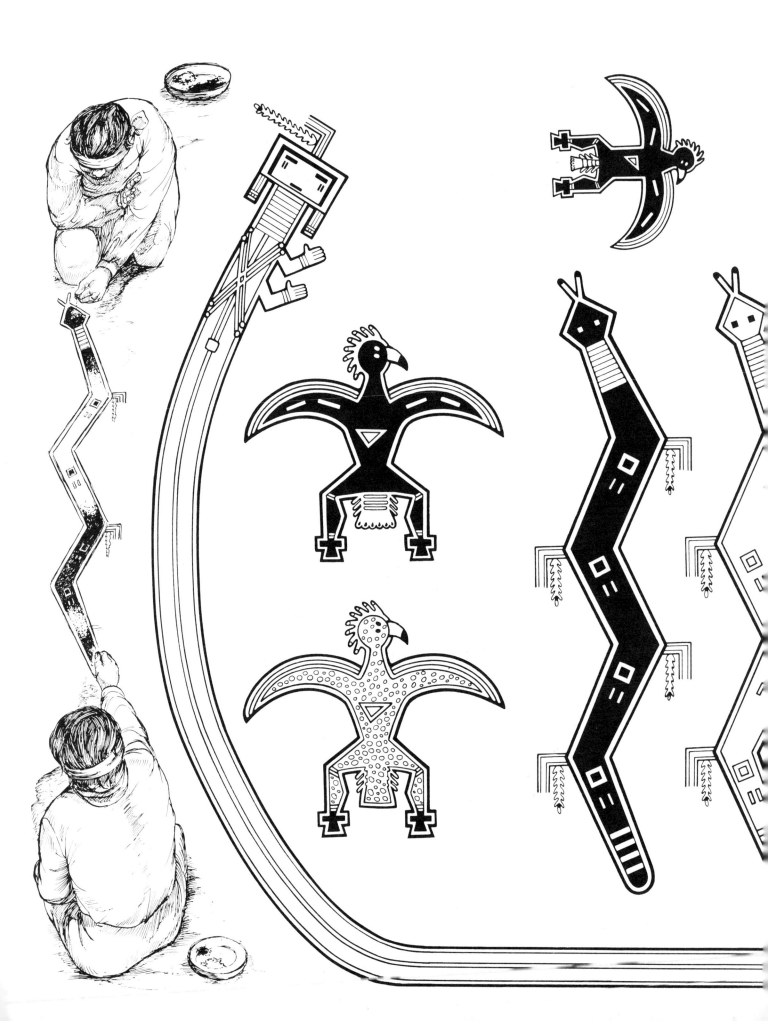

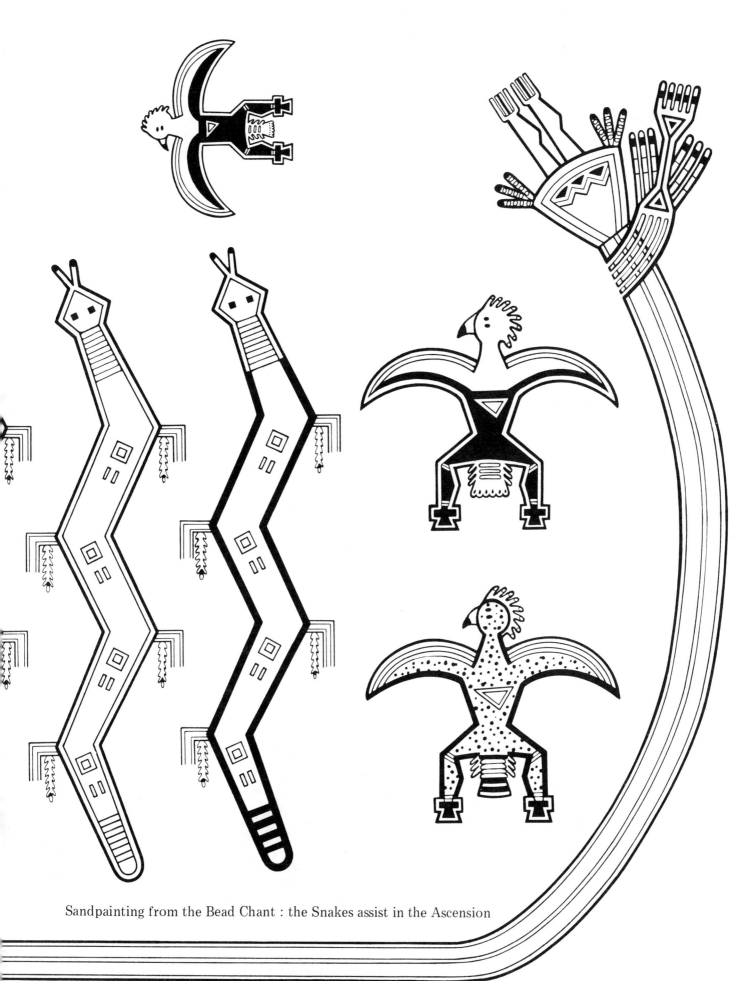

Sandpainting from the Bead Chant : the Snakes assist in the Ascension

After G. Reichard, 1939

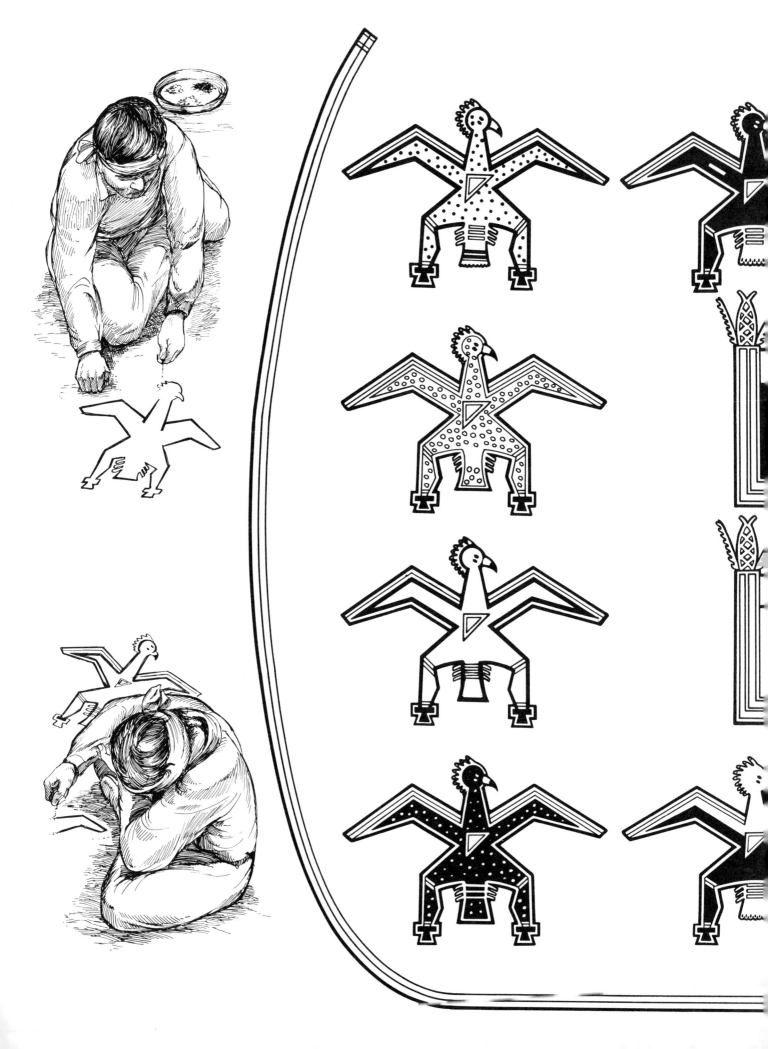

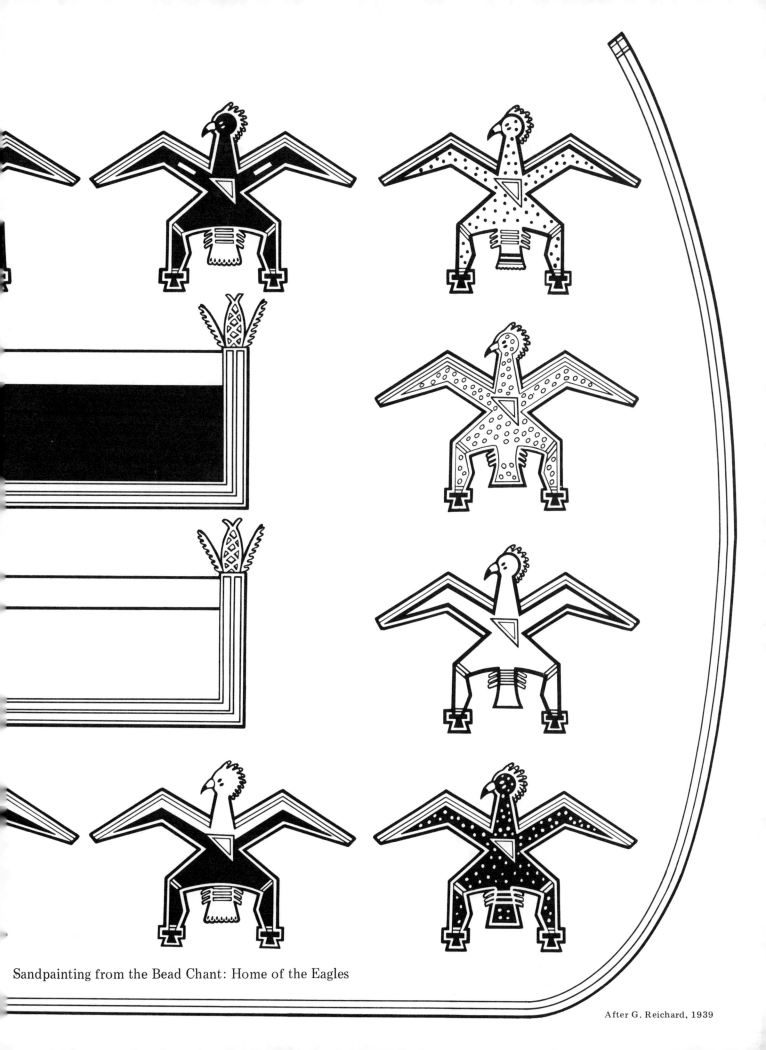

Sandpainting from the Bead Chant: Home of the Eagles

After G. Reichard, 1939

Mountain Lion was sent out as courier to invite people to a Beadway ceremony. On his journey he met Wolf who was giving invitations for another chant. So that everyone could attend both ceremonies, the two agreed upon different dates and sealed their agreement by exchanging quivers. However, on the day of the Bead ceremony, when the Pueblo people tried to trick his brother by substituting

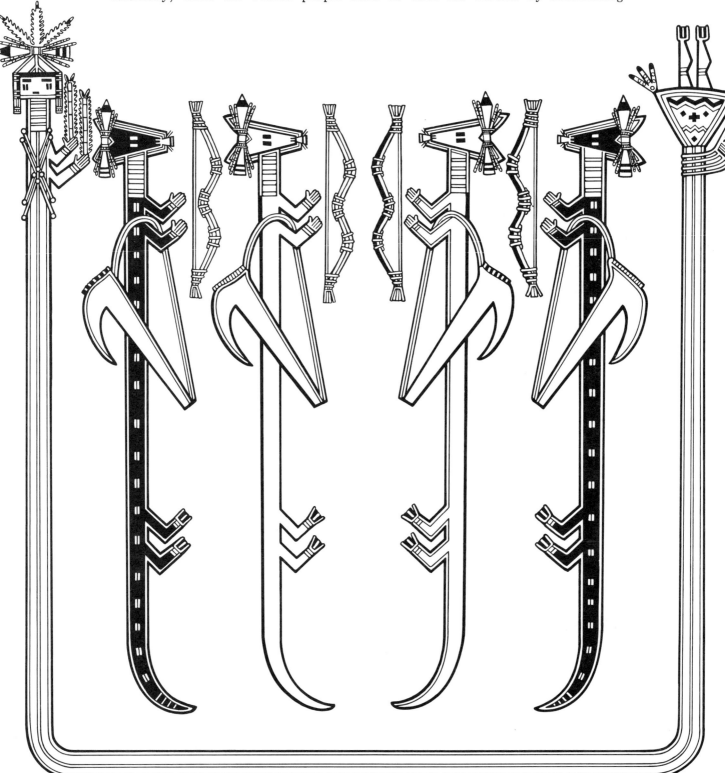

After G. Reichard, 1939

Sandpainting from the Bead Chant: Exchange of Quivers

imitation beads, Bead Boy returned and demanded real beads, which he took as payment for teaching the ceremony to his brother. (Ever since then medicine men have had to be paid for giving a ceremony.) At last two streaks of lightning lifted Bead Boy and with the aid of the eagles he rose to the sky to live with the Holy People.

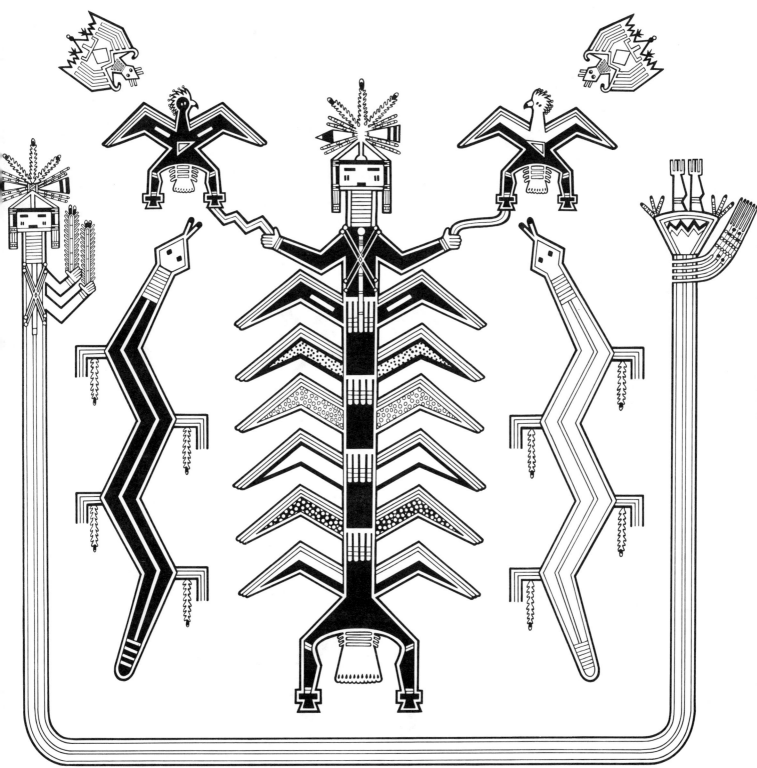

After G. Reichard, 1939

Sandpainting from the Bead Chant: Final Ascension Attended by Lightnings

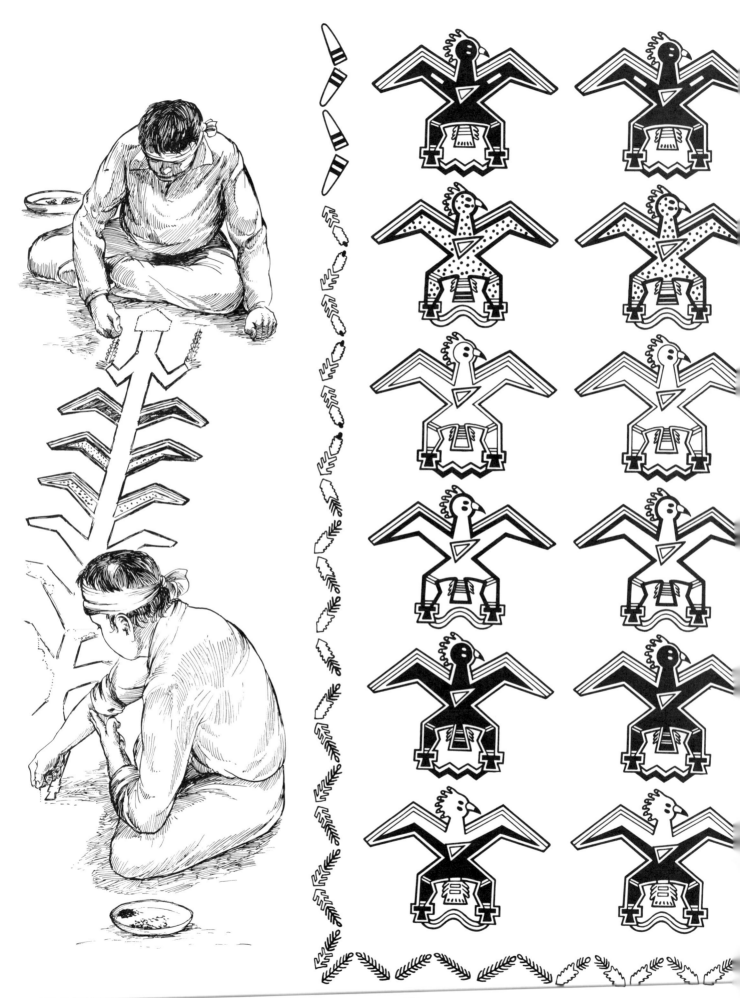

After G. Reichard, 1939

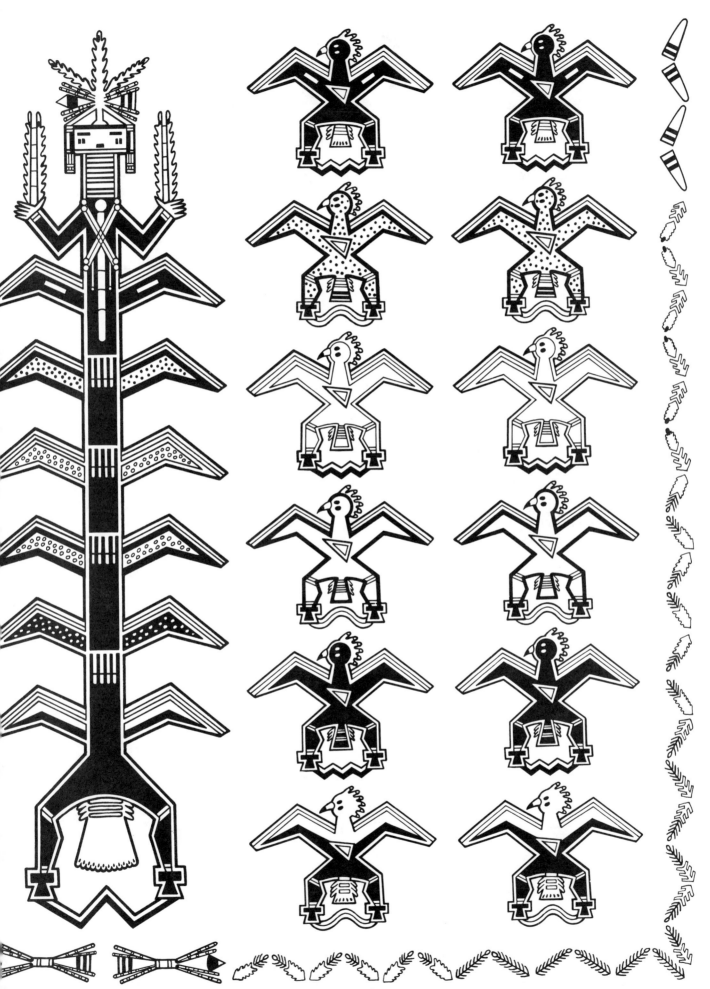

Sandpainting from the Bead Chant: Final Ascension Attended by Eagles

THE APACHE
The Gáhan—Mountain Spirits

Before the white man's day, certain bands of Indians who came to be called "Apaches" roamed over the Southwestern deserts and mountain heights. One of these bands was the Chiricahua Apache, who ranged down into northern Mexico. Before they were killed, or captured and placed on reservations established by the federal government, they were a numerous people. Their deities were called *Gáhan*, the Mountain Spirits. The old people had many stories to tell of them.

In the long ago, as they related, a baby boy was born without eyes in his face. Another baby boy was born without legs. As the Apache (like other Indians) always cared for the ill, elderly, orphans, and others in need, the people carried these two boys around until they were young men. Then they got tired of this chore.

They had no horses in those days, but they had to move to a distant region. The women had to carry great bundles, and they had to put their children atop the bundles. The two boys were too much of a burden, so the people left them and moved to the distant location. They left the boys a water jar filled with water, but they left them no food.

The boys discussed their plight. The one with legs said to the one with eyes, "I'll carry you and you watch where we are going. Tell me how to keep the trail and we'll follow the people." They started on the trail. They drank all their water and were dying of thirst when the Gáhan came to them.

The Gáhan took the boys to the mountain which was their home. Many people came together. "Many people lived in that mountain." And it is told that they "dressed all kinds of Mountain Spirits for these boys. They prayed and they began to sing." The women who lived in the mountain made the cry of applause, as they did in adolescence rites. The boys prayed to the Gahan. The blind one asked to see; the other one asked for legs.

Clouds appeared, and thunder and lightning. Black clouds covered the boys, so they became invisible. Then the black clouds vanished and the boys were there. The one who had lacked eyes now had eyes; the other boy had legs.

Many Gáhan were dancing. They asked the boys, "Would you like to go back to your own people now?" The boys said, "Yes." So the Gáhan instructed them to go to the top of a certain mountain near which their people were camped. They bade them to call the people and "tell them who you are, but don't let them come to you for four days."

The boys did as they were told. The people called back and asked, "Who are you?" When the boys told them, the people ran forth, but the boys made them stop. for four days. The people could hardly believe that these were the boys they had left behind. Then the boys called their fathers and mothers, and were recognized.

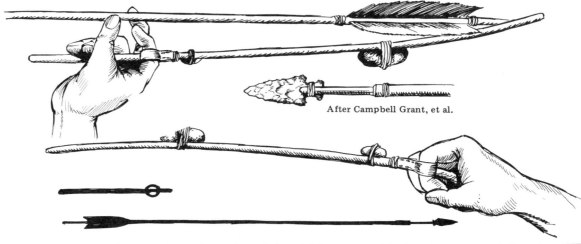

After Campbell Grant, et al.

The *atlatl,* or throwing stick, which was used before
the bow and arrow were introduced to the Southwest

The Navajo carried their dry paintings, or sandpaintings, to eminent heights of Southwestern Indian symbolic art, with efficacious medicinal rites and philosophical ceremonialism. The Apache made paintings of lesser extent and simpler ceremonies. Apache medicine men painted designs on skins, and they drew dry paintings upon the ground with colored earths during healing rites. As changes in life ways took place the Apache abandoned the making of these paintings.

They always attempted to picture objects literally rather than to represent them conventionally or symbolically. Here is illustrated an Apache sandpainting made nearly 100 years ago, at the time of a curing ceremony held for a paralytic patient. The medicine man in charge directed assistants in the making of this painting.

The sandpainting portrays the Mountain Spirits, or Gáhan, within a roughly drawn circle, one in each of the four directions. Each deity is shown wearing an elaborate mask and carrying two ceremonial wands. Attire is a short kilt and moccasins; on the bodies are painted decorations. The zig-zag lines are lightning symbols. The Gahan seen in ceremonies were men representing the real Gahan.

When the sandpainting was completed the medicine man took his position close to the figure of the east. At his right sat twelve selected singers with a drum. Four masked dancers stationed themselves at the cardinal points. The patient entered from the east and seated himself on the head of the central figure in the painting. As he sat down, the medicine man began to sing and the chorus joined in at once.

The singers sang in multiples of four—either singing a song four times or singing four songs, as the medicine man directed. When the songs were finished, the four masked Gáhan scraped the colored earths into a heap about the patient and rubbed his body with handsful of the earths. If the patient did not recover, it was taken as evidence that the gods did not will his curing.

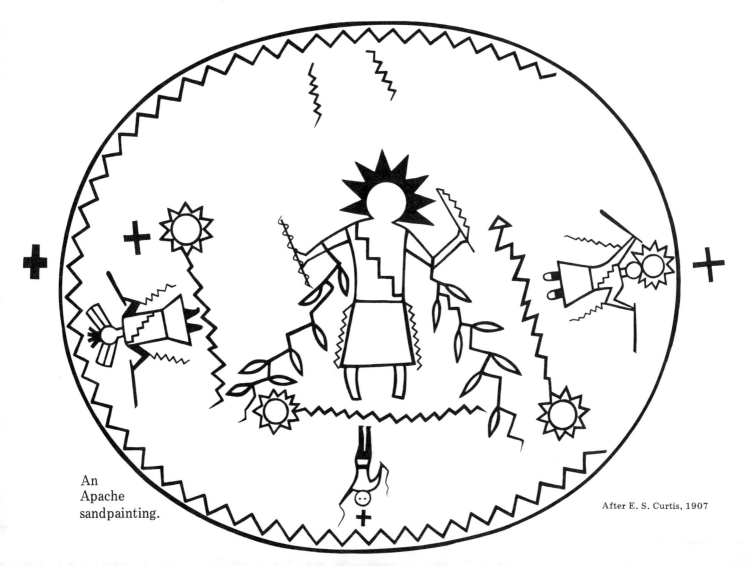

An
Apache
sandpainting.

After E. S. Curtis, 1907

AN APACHE PRAYER

addressed to White Painted Woman by the medicine man—

[White Painted Woman], you are good. I pray for a long life.

I pray for your good looks.

I pray for good breath.

I pray for good speech.

I pray for feet like yours to carry me through a long life.

I pray for a life like yours.

I walk with people; ahead of me all is well.

I pray for people to smile as long as I live.

I pray to live long.

I pray, I say, for a long life to live with you where the good people are.

I live in poverty.

I wish the people there to speak of goodness and to talk to me.

I wish you to divide your good things with me, as a brother.

Ahead of me is goodness, lead me on.

-from Curtis, E. S., 1907 Vol. I:37